kids draw™
DINOSAURS
CHRISTOPHER HART

WATSON-GUPTILL PUBLICATIONS/
NEW YORK

This book is dedicated to that fearless crew of dinosaur hunters: Glenn Heffernan, Harriet Pierce, Candace Raney, Alisa Palazzo, Julie Mazur, Ellen Greene, Bob Fillie, Hector Campbell, Charles Whang, Sheila Emery, Ali Kokmen, and Lee Wiggins.

Senior Editor: Candace Raney
Editor: Julie Mazur
Designer: Bob Fillie, Graphiti Design, Inc.
Production Manager: Hector Campbell
Text set in 12-pt Frutiger Roman

All drawings by Christopher Hart.
Inked tracings on pages 8–11, 34–39, 46, 56–57,
and 50–51 provided by Rich Faber.

Cover art by Christopher Hart
Text copyright © 2001 Art Studio, LLC
Illustrations copyright © 2001 Art Studio, LLC

First published in 2001 by
Watson-Guptill Publications,
a division of VNU Business Media, Inc.,
770 Broadway, New York, NY 10003
www.wgpub.com

Library of Congress Cataloging-in-Publication Data
Hart, Christopher.
    Kids draw dinosaurs / Christopher Hart.
        p. cm.
    Summary: Presents step-b y-step instructions for drawing dinosaurs, covering general tips, details of specific kinds of dinosaurs, and different styles.
    ISBN 0-8230-2689-2
    1. Dinosaurs in art—Juvenile literature. 2. Drawing—Technique—Juvenile literature. [1. Dinosaurs in art. 2. Drawing—Technique.] I. Title.

NC780.5 .H37 2001
743.6—dc21

                                            2001026569

Printed in China

First printing, 2001

2 3 4 5 6 7 8 / 08 07 06 05

CONTENTS

INTRODUCTION

Okay, dinosaur hunters, get ready to travel back in time—before the age of cars, before the wheel was invented, and yes, even before TV! It's hard to imagine, but long ago there were creatures as big as buildings, who could eat bedtime snacks the size of a horse. No, I'm not talking about your grandma—I'm talking about dinosaurs!

Just follow these lessons to draw some of the greatest dinosaurs that ever lived, from the awesome T-Rex to the lovable Triceratops. You'll also draw reptiles of the sea and sky, saber-toothed cats, woolly mammoths, and more. As you go, you'll pick up drawing skills, like how to build bodies with simple shapes and how to use *perspective* to make your dinosaurs look real.

All of the creatures in this book are *extinct.* This means they died out long ago. Scientists use bones and fossils to figure out their shapes and how they behaved. The only problem is, bones can't tell you what color an animal was, or what markings it had on its skin. Dinosaurs could have been brown, green, yellow, striped, or even polka-dotted! That part is up to you!

Even though I'm a cartoonist, the drawings in this book are based on real dinosaurs, how they looked and how they moved. But part of being a cartoonist is making your drawings *fun*. By drawing the dinosaurs rounder and with expressions on their faces, I've given each one its own personality. And you can, too!

So, are you ready to step into our time machine? Then let's go!

GETTING STARTED

Hi gang! Welcome aboard. Let's start by tackling a couple of easy basics. These techniques will help you draw the coolest dinosaurs ever to roam the face of the earth.

Dinosaur Bodies

The first trick to drawing dinosaurs is to use *ovals* for their bodies. An oval is like a circle that's been squashed. Never use a circle for a dinosaur body. Circles are too simple and plain. And dinosaurs are never plain!

CIRCLE

OVAL

See how this oval lies sideways? This is because plant-eaters like the Apatosaurus stood *parallel* to (or lined up with) the ground.

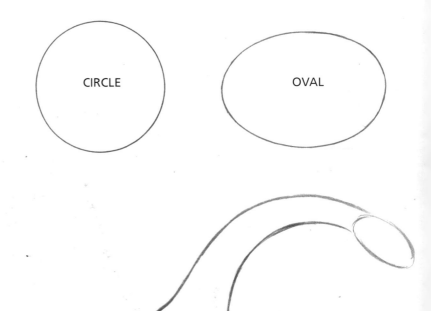

OVAL

The peaceful Apatosaurus

OVAL

See how this oval tilts upward? Most meat-eaters leaned forward as they walked. Their heels never touched the ground. They were so powerful, yet they walked on their tiptoes! Their tails stayed up in the air to balance their huge bodies.

The fearsome Tyrannosaurus Rex, or "T-Rex"

Tail stays up to balance its body.

Heels never touch the ground.

Dinosaur Heads

Most dinosaurs had heads that were long, but not that wide. Keep this in mind to help your dinosaurs look real—and scary!

LONG

SHORT

Here is the head of the powerful T-Rex. Its jawbones were big and strong, giving it incredible crushing power!

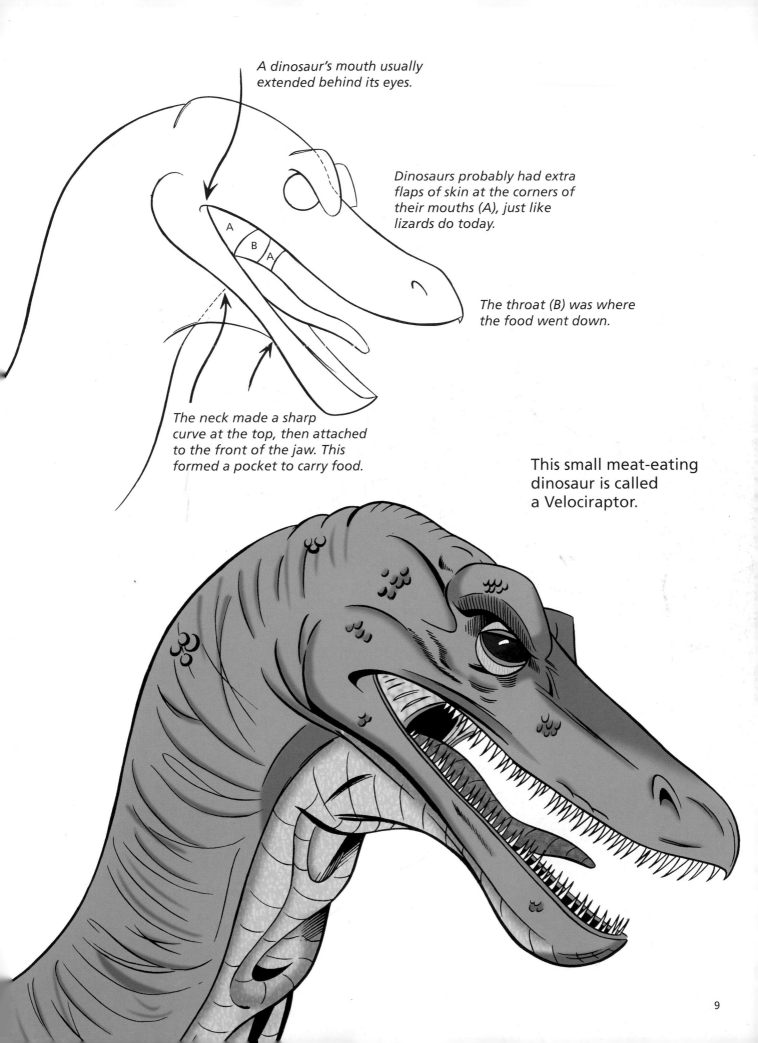

A dinosaur's mouth usually extended behind its eyes.

Dinosaurs probably had extra flaps of skin at the corners of their mouths (A), just like lizards do today.

The throat (B) was where the food went down.

The neck made a sharp curve at the top, then attached to the front of the jaw. This formed a pocket to carry food.

This small meat-eating dinosaur is called a Velociraptor.

Dinosaur Feet and Claws

Dinosaurs' feet were really cool. Some could kill an enemy with just one swipe.

T-REX
The T-Rex had three toes with sharp claws that scratched at the ground. Its fourth toe was higher up on the leg. It was really just a useless thumb.

APATOSAURUS
The Apatosaurus ate only plants. It was heavy and slow. Its feet had to be thick and sturdy to carry all its weight. Each foot had five toes, and its nails were not as sharp as on the meat-eaters.

Drawing Styles

I use three different styles when drawing dinosaurs: realistic, semi-realistic, and cartoony. Give each of them a try. Only *you* can decide which style is right for you!

REALISTIC
This is the best style for drawing scary dinosaurs. The trick is to take your time. Work carefully to fill in lots of details. Shading is important, too.

SEMI-REALISTIC
This style is still exciting, but less realistic. See how I've started to add some personality? This guy would make a great villain for an animated cartoon movie.

CARTOONY
This style is very simple, with big, bold lines. It's not at all realistic. You can add as much personality as you want!

The Line of Action

Many beginning artists draw their characters standing straight up. This makes their drawings look stiff. Don't be shy—make your dinosaurs really move!

How do you do this? First, make a quick, rough drawing (called a *sketch*) of the pose you want to do. Then draw an arrow through the pose. This is the *line of action.* It sets the direction of the pose. If your arrow is straight, your pose is too stiff. If the arrow turns and curves boldly, then you've got a great action pose!

Let's Draw!

Time to try drawing a dinosaur from scratch. This one is a Megalosaurus, which was a *predator.* That means it was a meat-eating hunter.

First, build the basic body. Use ovals and other simple shapes. Test your pose with a line of action.

Erase extra lines and blend the shapes together.

Add markings to the skin. Draw details like the eyes, mouth, and teeth.

Add color, and you're done!

PLANT-EATERS

Plant-eaters came in an amazing variety of shapes and sizes. Many of them were huge—much bigger than the fierce meat-eaters.

Apatosaurus

The Apatosaurus is thought to have been very big and very heavy, weighing about 33 tons (that's 66 *thousand* pounds, to be exact!). It had a long neck and tail. Its hind legs had to be powerful to lift its huge body off the ground so it could eat leaves and flowers on the treetops.

Draw two overlapping circles. Add a long neck.

Connect the circles. Add the tail. (This drawing has only part of the tail.)

Add massive legs and arms. Wrap the arms in layers of fat. This boy was a big eater, that's for sure!

Use lots of
sketchy lines to
make the skin
look tough and
hard. Shade it
with your pencil,
or use colors.

The Apatosaurus might have liked to play in water,
which would have lightened its great weight.
There would have been lots of plants to eat by the
water's edge, too.

Duck-billed Dinosaurs

Duck-billed dinosaurs lived in groups, or *herds.* They survived over a long period of time and roamed large areas of the earth, including North America. Isn't it strange to think that dinosaurs might have lived in your own backyard?

There were many types of duck-billed dinosaurs. Most had similar bodies, but an amazing variety of crowns on their heads. Here are some examples. Which do you like best? My favorite is the Parasaurolophus. Don't feel bad. I can't pronounce it, either!

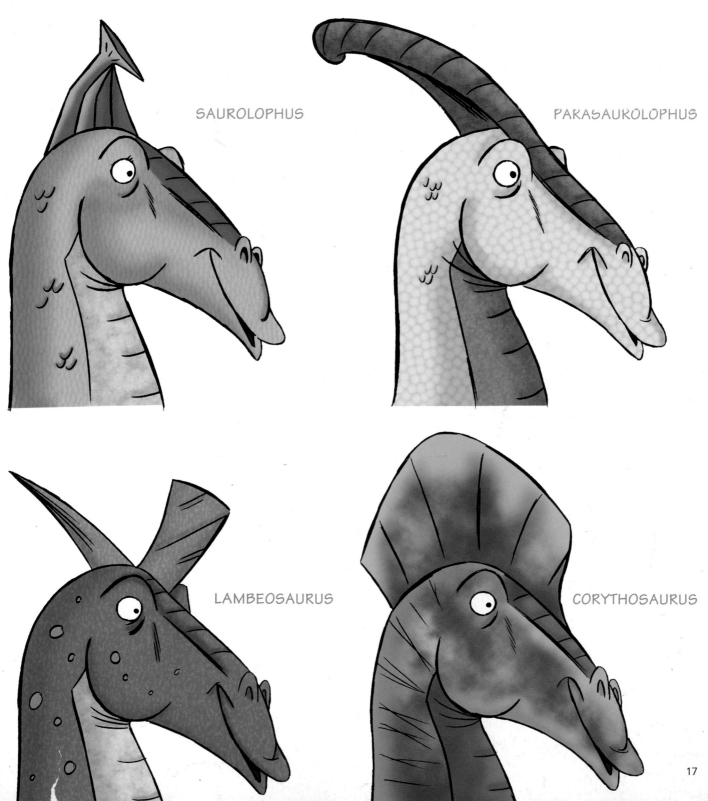

SAUROLOPHUS

PARASAUROLOPHUS

LAMBEOSAURUS

CORYTHOSAURUS

TSINTAOSAURUS

This odd-looking duck-billed dinosaur was from China.
It was about three to four times as tall as a human!
And what is that weird horn on its head? Well,
scientists aren't quite sure. Some believe that the fossil
bones weren't put together right, and that the horn
doesn't even belong there. Mistakes can happen, even
with scientists. Fossils don't come with instructions!

SMALL
CHEST
AREA

LARGE
BOTTOM
AREA

THICK TAIL

Trees were the only fast-food restaurants in those days!

One kind of duck-billed dinosaur was the Hypacrosaurus.

The face narrows to a tiny nose and chin.

19

EDMONTOSAURUS

The Edmontosaurus was another duck-billed dinosaur. They probably had to drink quickly and stay alert, because hungry predators would have hidden near the water waiting for thirsty victims to come along.

Stegosaurus

Even a slow giant such as the Stegosaurus had a secret weapon. Just look at those spikes! And see those big plates on its back? They made it hard to get a good bite of "Steggy" from above. This might—just might—have caused an attacker to go after someone else instead.

The back is very curvy, but the tummy is drawn with a straight line. The neck is thin and the head is so tiny that it's almost funny. This is why I like to draw Steggy in a cartoon style.

Add the legs and the eyeball.

Add plates on Steggy's back and spikes on its tail. Draw a line where the arrows are to show where the tough outer skin changes to the soft underbelly.

Triceratops

The Triceratops always reminds me of a rhinoceros, with its horns and low, compact body. It used the crown of its head like a shield, to protect itself against attack.

Here's a trick to make drawing the crown easier: Draw a curved line for the top of the head. Then draw a jagged line *over* your curved line. To finish, erase the curved line.

Armor-Plated Dinosaurs

Some dinosaurs were covered with plates of armor. One look at these guys and you know what a tough world they must have lived in!

Start with an oval shape for the body. Add the tail and a tiny head.

TALARURUS

The Talarurus had armor *plus* nasty spikes. And look at that tail! Can you imagine the headache a predator would get if hit over the head with that thing?

Add elephant-like feet.

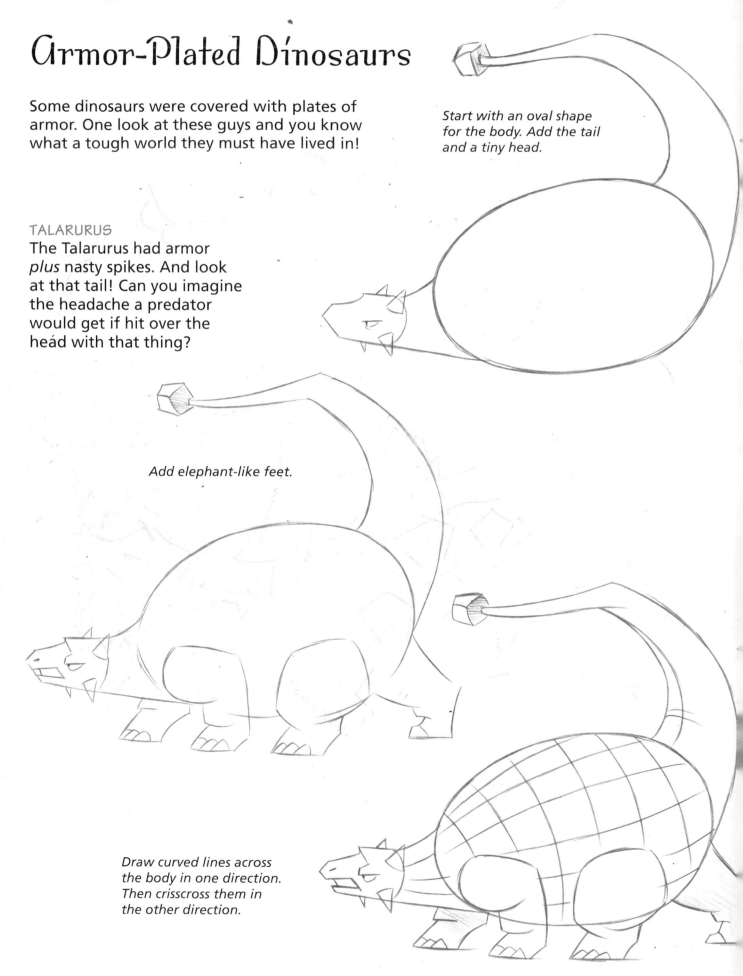

Draw curved lines across the body in one direction. Then crisscross them in the other direction.

Add spikes and some texture
to the tail and skin. Draw
details on the face. Add color,
and you're done!

DESMATOSUCHUS

The armor-plated Desmatosuchus had spikes that faced *backwards*! It probably used these to back up into its enemies, giving them an unpleasant surprise.

Like any good cartoonist, I've made these spikes look *extra* dangerous. They may not be perfectly realistic, but aren't they cool?!

Armor-plated dinosaurs had armor to protect their backs, but their soft bellies were still vulnerable. They had to curl up or stay on their feet at all times.

This Megalosaurus is having second thoughts. Maybe it'd better skip lunch today!

THE GREAT MEAT-EATERS

Nothing is as awesome as a hungry meat-eating dinosaur! These chilling creatures usually had low foreheads, long faces, and *lots* of sharp teeth. Their arms were tiny and almost useless. But their legs were thick, sturdy, and powerful.

Tyrannosaurus Rex

The dreaded Tyrannosaurus Rex, or T-Rex, was the baddest boy of the Late Cretaceous Period.

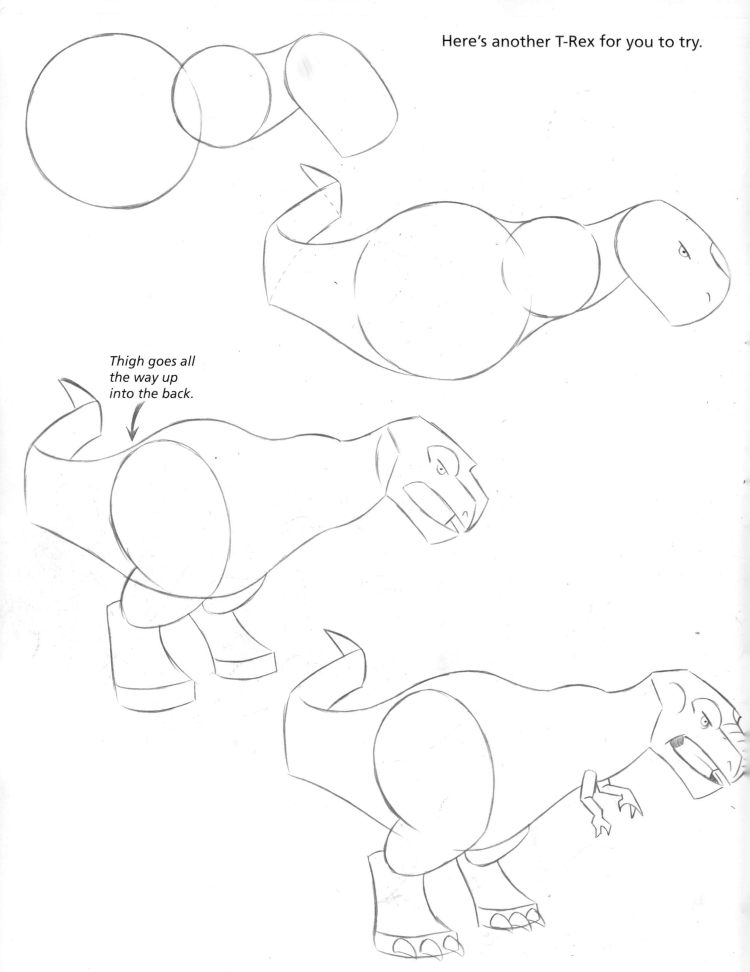

Here's another T-Rex for you to try.

Thigh goes all the way up into the back.

Megalosaurus

The Megalosaurus was another great meat-eater. It had a slightly pointier face than the T-Rex.

I think this Megalosaurus should be striped. What do you think?

Spinosaurus

The Spinosaurus was huge. It measured almost 50 feet from the end of its tail to the tip of its nose!

Draw the neck like an "s." The body is just a simple egg shape.

Add the big fan on the back.

Draw thick legs that stand on two toes. And how about some sharp teeth to go with that evil smile?

Add texture to the skin. Color, and you're done!

DINOSAUR WARS!

Dinosaurs had armor plates, horned heads and tails, and razor-sharp teeth and claws. Why did they need such heavy-duty equipment? Because life on primeval earth was full of fierce battles for survival.

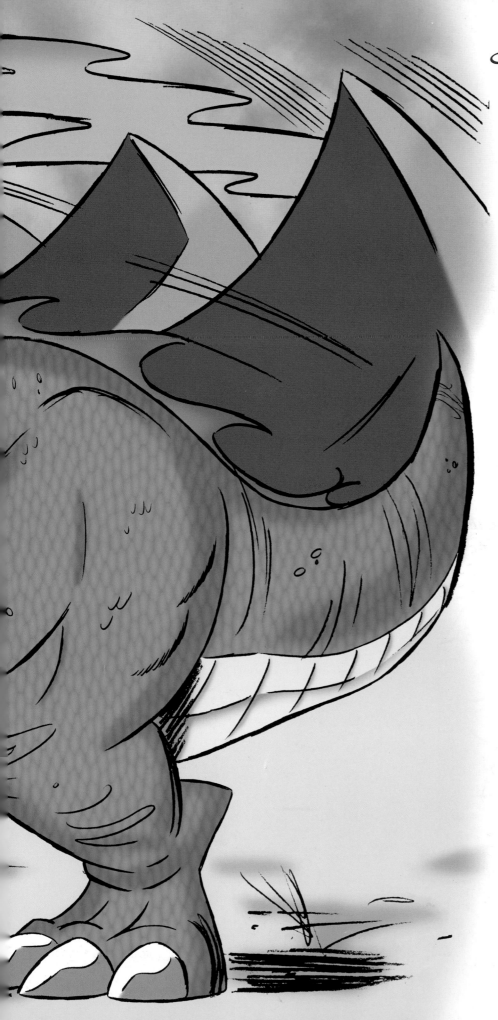

T-Rex Versus Triceratops

You'd think it would be easy for the mighty T-Rex to defeat the smaller, slower Triceratops. But old Triceratops had a few tricks of his own. He was low to the ground, so he could get under T-Rex's soft underbelly. And those horns on the Triceratops's head were long and *very* sharp. Just one wrong move and it's all over—for either of our two warriors!

Two Giants Battle for Survival

These two T-Rex titans are circling each other, looking for a chance to attack. One moment's hesitation could mean death for either one!

The weaker T-Rex lets down its guard for only a second, but that's all it takes.

Pack Hunters

Some smaller meat-eaters may have hunted in packs. That was the only way they could take down a great dinosaur, like the Apatosaurus.

By the way, this drawing could never have really happened. The Apatosaurus went extinct about 40 million years before the smaller dinosaur, Deinonychus, was even around! In comics, cartoons, and animation, artists sometimes fudge these things to make scenes more exciting.

On the Hunt

When the ground rumbles and quakes, you know the terrible T-Rex is near. And if he's just woken up hungry, you'd better run... *fast*!

Actually, some scientists think that the T-Rex may not have been such a ferocious hunter after all. It may have been more of a *scavenger*, eating food other dinosaurs had already killed instead of doing the hunting itself.

ANCIENT REPTILES

If you thought dinosaurs were weird, wait 'til you see these crazy reptiles. Believe it or not, some of them were around even *before* dinosaurs!

Dunkleosteus

Some ancient reptiles lived in the water, such as this eel-like Dunkleosteus. It was covered in armor for protection.

Placodus

Scientists think the Placodus ate shellfish and had very sharp teeth. It had a thick body and a small head. And don't forget the ridges on its back.

Ichthyosaurus

The Icthyosaurus looked kind of like a shark, with a huge stomach and a long, thin nose. Notice how the mouth goes behind the eyes.

Plesiosaurus

The creatures that lived in the ocean 150 million years ago looked quite different from the friendly dolphins, goldfish, and turtles of today. Take a look at this Plesiosaurus, for example. Do you think its neck is long enough?

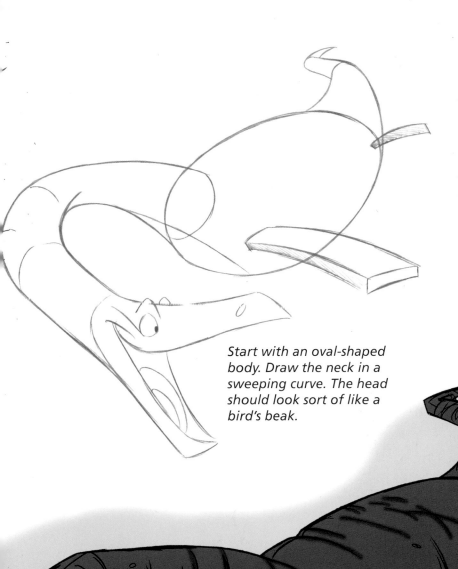

Start with an oval-shaped body. Draw the neck in a sweeping curve. The head should look sort of like a bird's beak.

Ptrenodon

Ptrenodons were actually flying reptiles. Sounds gross, right? It gets grosser. They had wings made of skin! Their arms were attached to the insides of their wings.

See the long plume on its head? No one knows if this really existed. Ancient animals may have had all sorts of decorations that we don't know about. As artists, we're free to use our imagination. To plume or not to plume—it's up to you!

The arms were long, to power those big wings.

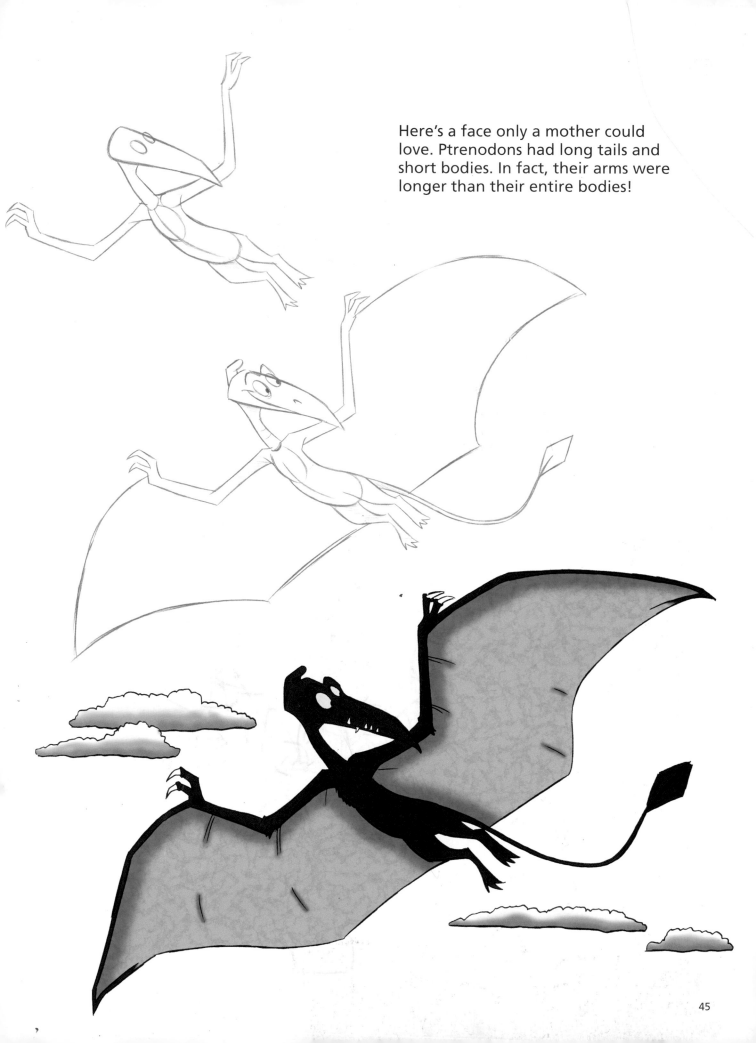

Here's a face only a mother could love. Ptrenodons had long tails and short bodies. In fact, their arms were longer than their entire bodies!

Edaphosaurus

The Edaphosaurus was an early lizard. It was very low to the ground, with a long body and short legs. And look at that cool fan on its back!

As you draw, follow the first steps *carefully*. Don't rush to do the details. Your drawing will look much better if the basics are done right.

Longisquama

If I saw this thing running around in my back yard, I'd call pest control in a *hurry*.

Here's the most important thing to remember when drawing the Longisquama:

Start by drawing the *entire* shape of its back spines first. Then split the shape into the separate spines. Last, decorate the spines with a design.

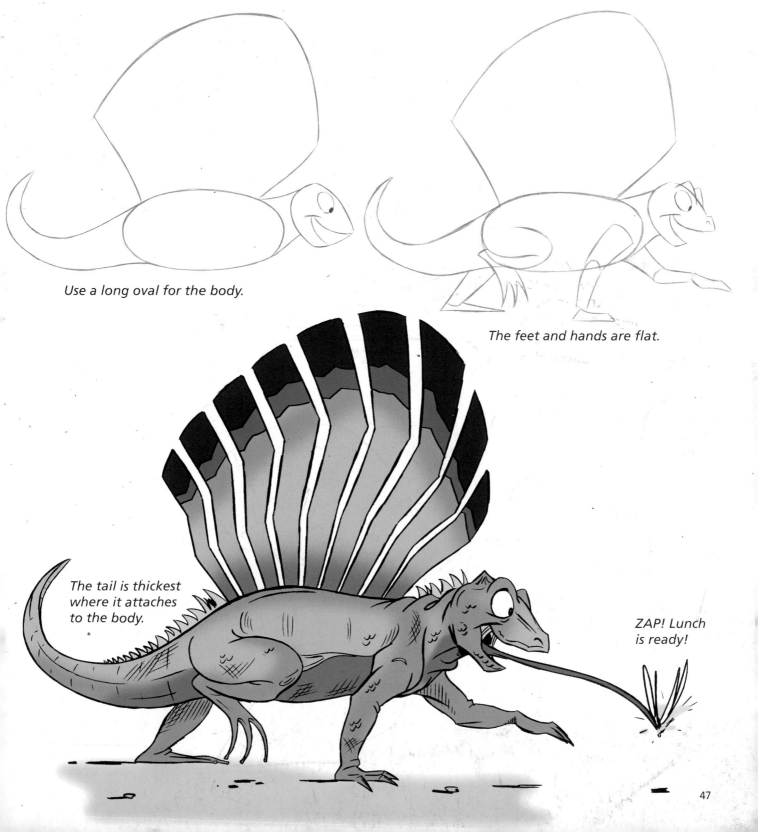

Use a long oval for the body.

The feet and hands are flat.

The tail is thickest where it attaches to the body.

ZAP! Lunch is ready!

Scutosaurus

The armor-plated Scutosaurus lived in Europe. Scientists think this guy moved very slowly, like most reptiles we see today.

As you try this drawing, think about the overlapping shapes. Shapes *overlap* when one lies on top of another. Parts of the body that are *closer* to you should overlap parts that are farther away. This creates the illusion of depth. It will help your drawings look more real.

See how the head overlaps the shoulders? See how the big part of the body overlaps the bent knee, and the knee overlaps the tail?

The spine curves to make the dinosaur look round. And notice how the right foot overlaps the arm?

Add details, like
the fingernails
and eyebrows.

Add horns on the face.
Make a few lines to show
wrinkles on the skin.
You've got it!

49

EARLY MAMMALS

Mammals around at the time of the dinosaurs were probably small, the size of mice. It wasn't until millions of years later, when the dinosaurs went extinct, that some of them became larger mammals like these (and, eventually, you and me!).

Saber-toothed Cat

No one ever said "Here, kitty, kitty" to this guy! When you draw the saber-toothed cat, use a slinky, winding pose. Look how the line of action goes through my drawing. It curves from the tip of the tail all the way to the head.

Stick one paw out in front. Make it really big for a dramatic pose.

The shoulders poke up over the arch of the back. This happens with most modern mammals, too.

Did Something Really Look Like This?

Believe it or not, something *did* look like this—the Embolotherium. It had a huge horn that fit right on its forehead. But aside from this weird headgear, its body wasn't all that different from many of today's larger African mammals.

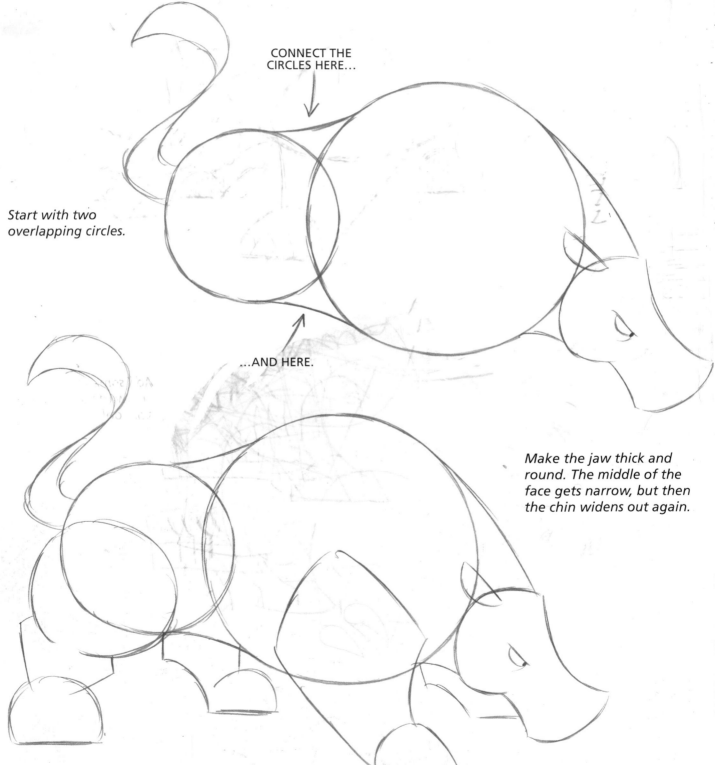

CONNECT THE CIRCLES HERE...

Start with two overlapping circles.

...AND HERE.

Make the jaw thick and round. The middle of the face gets narrow, but then the chin widens out again.

Add some rough lines
and warts to make the
skin look rugged.

Woolly Mammoth

Here he is, King of the Arctic North! Giant ancestor of the modern elephant! The woolly mammoth was a gigantic mammal, with tremendous tusks and powerful shoulders.

   See how the front legs look longer than the back legs, even though we know they're the same size? This is because of *perspective.* This is a law in art that says things closer to you will look larger than things farther away. The front legs are closer to you, so they should look larger.

The trunk dangles way down near the ground.

Draw humps where the shoulders stick up.

54

Add fur flapping in the wind to make the picture more exciting. Be sure all the fur flaps in the same direction. Wind usually blows one direction at a time.

Man Versus Beast

Most prehistoric creatures died out before the dawn of humans, but the last woolly mammoths may have died only 4,000 years ago—when the Egyptians were building their great pyramids.

Humans may have hunted the mammoths to extinction. The mammoth was giant, but it was no match for the human brain. Early people made weapons that eventually conquered these huge beasts.

The mammoths' tusks were used to build shelters. Hides were used for clothing. And their meat could feed an entire tribe of cave people through a long, hard winter.

DINOSAUR CARTOONS

Dinosaurs can be awesome and fascinating, but they can also be silly! Let's try drawing some fun dinosaur cartoons.

Gulp!

This Triceratops just noticed some unwanted company. Look at how I've exaggerated its mouth, tongue, and eyes. See how far you can stretch the expressions in your cartoons.

Dumb T-Rex

What makes this T-Rex look so harmless? The secret is his big bottom.

See the huge foot coming right at you? You can't see the leg behind it, even though you know it's there. This is because of a principle called *foreshortening.* Foreshortening is a way of showing how shapes come toward you in space. When this happens, the shape seems to block whatever is behind it.

Silly Plant-eater

This happy-go-lucky Apatosaurus is based on large shapes and long lines. Cartoonists sometimes break the rules by sticking the eyes on top of the head. I've even given this guy floating eyebrows.

What's for Dinner?

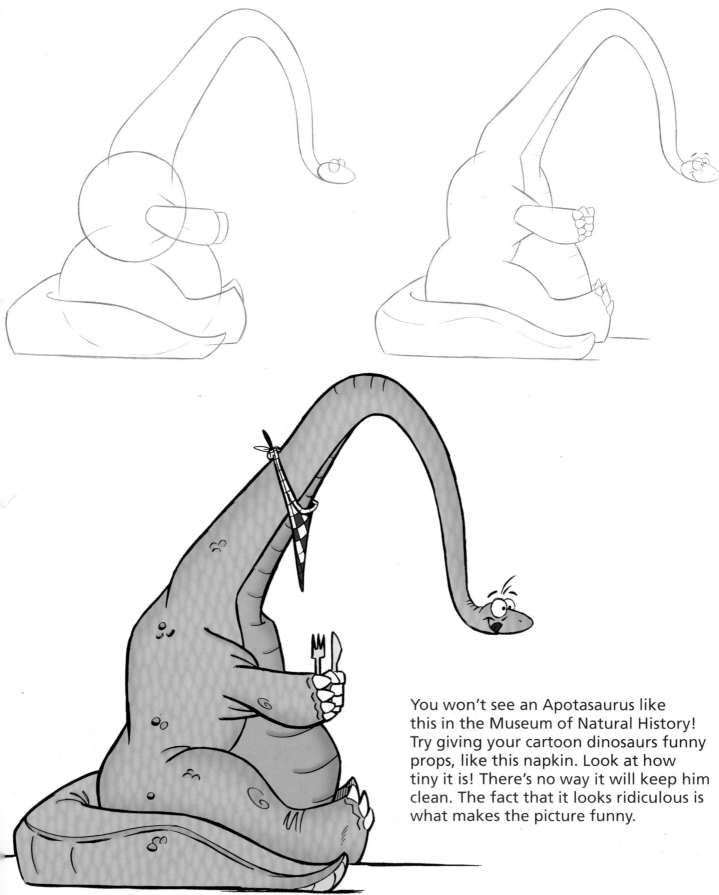

You won't see an Apotasaurus like this in the Museum of Natural History! Try giving your cartoon dinosaurs funny props, like this napkin. Look at how tiny it is! There's no way it will keep him clean. The fact that it looks ridiculous is what makes the picture funny.

Grumpy and Green

Ever have one of those days? This dinosaur's flat head and flat, single eyebrow give him a grumpy, funny look. I've made his already tiny arms even tinier. And instead of making his legs thicker at the *top*, as they should be, I've made them thickest at the *bottom*. Changing things like that makes a drawing funnier.

It's Still a Mystery

Dinosaurs and dragons look alike in many ways. Is this just a coincidence? Maybe not. Some people think that the idea of dragons came from early man's memories of dinosaurs. Maybe over the years, these grew into stories of dragons. But wait a minute—humans weren't around during the time of the dinosaurs. So how could they remember something they never saw? (Here's a hint: It has to do with old bones!)

Index